MARKET–FRESH MIXOLOGY

COCKTAILS
for
EVERY
SEASON

BRIDGET ALBERT WITH **MARY BARRANCO**

REVISED AND EXPANDED
SECOND EDITION

SURREY
BOOKS

AN AGATE IMPRINT

CHICAGO

Printed in China.

First trade paperback edition
March 2014
ISBN-10: 1-57284-159-1
ISBN-13: 978-1-57284-159-8

641.874

The Library of Congress has cataloged the first edition of this book as follows:

Library of Congress Cataloging-in-Publication Data
Albert, Bridget.
Market-fresh mixology : cocktails for every season / Bridget Albert with Mary Barranco.
    p. cm.
Includes index.
ISBN-13: 978-1-57284-095-9 (hardcover)
ISBN-10: 1-57284-095-1 (hardcover)
1. Cocktails. I. Barranco, Mary. II. Title.
TX951.A33 2008
641.8'74--dc22
                    2008009547

10 9 8 7 6 5 4 3 2 1

Surrey Books is an imprint of Agate Publishing. Agate books are available in bulk at discount prices. For more information, go to agatepublishing.com.

We dedicate this
book to our children,
Paige, Allison, and
Michael.

CONTENTS

FOREWORD

Fresh ingredients are like fresh ideas—they instill a sense of excitement and levity in the everyday, elevating even the simplest concepts to greatness.

Fresh ideas are the backbone of my work, as well as that of the entire culinary industry, with which my organization, Share Our Strength, works hand-in-hand to end childhood hunger in America. For more than 25 years, chefs, mixologists, and others in the culinary industry have shared their strengths and talents to help us connect kids to the healthy food they need, every day.

Bridget Albert, the creative palate behind *Market-Fresh Mixology*, is a longstanding supporter of Share Our Strength's No Kid Hungry® campaign. She understands that, just as it takes the best, freshest ingredients to create a great dish or drink, it takes the best, healthiest foods to help our kids grow and thrive.

Cheers,
Debbie Shore
Co-founder
Share Our Strength

ACKNOWLEDGMENTS

special thank you from my heart to my husband, Jamie; our daughter, Paige; my brother, Brian; my sister-in-law, Kasia; my parents, Nancy and David; and my Grandma Rosella. Thank you for your words of encouragement. Thank you, also, to my in-laws, aunts, uncles, cousins, and friends, who were the finest taste-testers. Finally, a warm thank you to my mentor, teacher, and friend, Tony Abou-Ganim.

Cheers,
Bridget

Thanks to my wonderful family, especially my husband, Joe; our children, Michael and Allison; my sisters, Teresa and Cathy, who are also my best friends and constant source of courage; and, last but not least, my brother Peter, who can fix anything.

Mary

We both extend gratitude to our work family and employer, Southern Wine & Spirits of Illinois, and our general manager, Will Conniff, who provides the format for us to bring our passion to the trade.

We also extend a special thank you to the members of the United States Bartenders Guild, for their dedication and drive in raising the bar.

"Fresh fruit is not enough. Finding local fruit that is picked off the tree when it is ripe is superior. It provides better taste that explodes in a subtle way. This means finding a local farm you trust. The winter is a challenge...we have to rely on the in-season fruits we get from California and Florida..."

BOB PALLOTTA
SLOW FOOD CHAIRMAN

"Farmers welcome each season. We look forward to planting in the spring, summer growth, and fall harvest. Winter is a time for us to rest and reflect on the year before. We look to Mother Nature to provide everything else."

FARMER JOHN THOMPSON

MORRIS, ILLINOIS

INTRODUCTION

Whether you are entertaining a large crowd, hosting a cocktail party, or spending the evening with a close friend, a *cocktail* is meant to be savored.

Like fine wines, a memorable cocktail needs layers of flavor. **My only rule is that cocktails must be balanced with freshness.** This book will show you each step in making these simple, fresh, and modern cocktails, as you learn to enhance the classics. Great classics, such as the Mojito, which emerged in the mid 1900s, are making the scene again for your sipping pleasure. One of my favorite twists on this classic, the Blueberry Lavender Mojito, adds a splash of culinary freshness and creativity.

All great recipes require the basics. Up front, you'll find a section on *Home Bar Essentials*, which gives you the fundamentals of cocktail creation with a quick reference outlining the right spirits, store-bought and homemade mixers, tools, and glassware needed to complete each cocktail. As you read on in the book, you'll see that each recipe includes an easy-to-follow format, with a *Tool Box* of supplies for every recipe.

The changing seasons are the inspiration for every recipe in *Market-Fresh Mixology*, including the spring-fresh Rhubarb Strawberry Collins and the winter-savory Caviar Martini. These recipes feature your favorite spirits, like vodka, tequila, gin, bourbon, or sparkling wine for celebration cocktails, mixed with delicious ingredients from each chapter's *Season's Best* list of flavorful in-season produce.

In the final chapter, you'll learn the art of making cocktail infusions, such as Bing Cherries with Cinnamon and Bourbon. Infusions capture the spirits and flavors of the season as they meld together over time.

As you read through, enjoy the tidbits of cocktail lore and historic drinking toasts. I'm sure they will inspire you to make the freshest cocktails the season has to offer. Let's raise the bar as we raise our glasses. Cheers!

HOME
BAR
ESSENTIALS

TOOLS OF THE TRADE

Just like an artist needs a paintbrush, paint, and a canvas, there are a few basic tools for the home bartender. Making consistently great cocktails requires the freshest ingredients and key essentials, such as the shaker, strainer, muddler, and bar spoon. Like most home goods, these tools are available for a wide range of prices, depending on the quality. The next few pages outline some bar-tool necessities.

Shakers

There are two basic styles to choose from.

Boston shaker: A two-piece shaker consisting of a tin and a pint glass. A separate strainer is required. The Boston shaker is most often selected by classic bartenders and is a personal favorite.

Cobbler: A three-piece metal cocktail shaker with a built-in strainer and a cap.

Strainers

Hawthorn strainer: A metal strainer designed to fit over the top of a cocktail shaker to strain the drink into the glass. Has 2-4 prongs, and a spring around the outer edge that fits over the cocktail shaker. Controls the speed of the pour while keeping ice in the shaker.

Julep strainer: A strainer that is placed over the glass of a Boston shaker to remove ice and strain the cocktail. Similar in appearance to a slotted spoon and most often used for bourbon cocktails that are traditionally stirred in the pint glass of a shaker.

Other Tools

Bar spoon: A long spoon with a twisted handle used to stir cocktails directly in a serving glass or the pint glass of the Boston shaker.

Muddler: A small club used to crush, mash, or grind ingredients in order to release essential flavors and oils. The muddler is placed directly in the cocktail or pint glass, and it is used with motions similar to those used with a mortar and pestle.

Citrus press: A hand-held juicer designed to extract juice from citrus fruit.

Citrus peeler: A thin, sharp tool used to separate a citrus fruit's peel from its pith. (Most often used for making garnishes.)

Jigger: A double-sided liquid measuring tool with a jigger (which measures 1½ ounces) on one side and a pony (which measures 1 ounce) on the reverse side.

Zester/grater: A utensil with sharp raised areas that is used to grate small pieces of fruit or spices.

Corkscrew: An apparatus with a handle and a sharp metal spiral that is used to remove corks from wine bottles. A waiter's corkscrew also has a small blade to cut the foil on a wine bottle.

Bottle opener: A device used to remove the caps from some beer and soda bottles.

Sieve: A metal utensil made of mesh that is used to separate particles from liquid. Traditionally, a bartender-size sieve is 2 to 3 inches in diameter.

Paring knife: A short-bladed knife used to peel and slice fruit and vegetables.

Cutting board: A small, washable surface will suffice for most bars.

Other necessities include:

Bar towel

Ice bucket and scoop

Cocktail napkins

Cocktail picks

Glassware Suggestions

One of the most often-asked questions about cocktails and home bartending is not only what to serve, but how best to serve it. Every well-stocked bar should have the appropriate glassware for cocktail, wine, and beer service. Your choices in glassware style and costs are unlimited. Once you have the basics, as outlined here, you can continue to add interesting specialty glasses, including brandy snifters, cordial glasses, and fun collectibles.

The next question you need to consider is the quantity to purchase. Analyze your entertainment style. Do you host large events with many guests, or are you more likely to have cozy gatherings? At minimum, have six of each of these basics on hand, and select styles that have been in production for some time and are likely to continue to be available, so you can add more later if necessary.

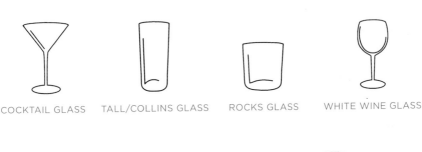

COCKTAIL GLASS   TALL/COLLINS GLASS   ROCKS GLASS   WHITE WINE GLASS

RED WINE GLASS   CHAMPAGNE FLUTE   PINT GLASS FOR BEER

Spirits, Wine, and Beer

Having a well-stocked bar ensures guest satisfaction, no matter the request. The Home Bar Essentials *Spirit List* gives basic product suggestions and descriptions. Be sure to have on hand at least one selection in each spirit category. Later, add items like mezcal or rye whiskey to create variety and enhance the flavors of your crafted cocktails. Customize your bar by adding neighborhood favorites like beer from local breweries.

SPIRIT LIST

Vodka: A neutral spirit without a distinctive taste, aroma, character, or color. Flavored vodkas can enhance cocktails, and many enjoy citrus-flavored vodkas in particular.

Gin: A distilled spirit, with its main flavors coming from juniper and other botanicals.

Rum: A spirit made from sugar cane, sugar cane syrup, or molasses that can be matured and blended. White and dark rum are the bar basics. Other styles include:

- Golden
- Añejo, vieux, age-dated
- Spiced, flavored

Tequila: A distinctive product of Mexico that is derived principally from the agave tequilana weber ("blue" variety) plant. The following styles are widely available.

- Silver/bianco (unaged)
- Reposado (aged for at least 2 months)
- Añejo (aged for up to 12 months)

A silver tequila is unaged and therefore has a simple flavor. It is a blank canvas suitable for most margaritas. Match the bold flavors of aged tequilas with heartier fruits and cocktails.

Scotch whisky: A product of Scotland, manufactured in compliance with the laws of the United Kingdom. If it is a mixture of whiskies, it's labeled a "blended Scotch whisky." A single-malt Scotch comes from a single distillery in Scotland and is made from or of malted barley. Best consumed straight up or on the rocks.

One blended Scotch and one single-malt from the Highlands will suffice as you begin to build your bar inventory. Explore regions like Islay and the Lowlands as you expand into a wider style and taste variety in single-malts.

Whiskey, whisky, and bourbon: All a basic bar needs is one favorite bourbon and one favorite rye whiskey. Experiment with a variety of other selections over time.

- American whiskey: This whiskey is made in the United States from a grain mash and aged in oak.
- Bourbon whiskey: Bourbon is produced only in the United States and made from 51% corn mash and Kentucky spring water. If it is less than 4 years old, its age must be displayed on the bottle.
- Canadian whisky: Canadian whisky (note that it does not include the "e" in the spelling) derives from a mash of various grains and is aged in oak for three years.
- Corn whiskey: At least 80% of this whiskey's mash is corn.
- Rye whiskey: This whiskey is predominantly rye mash and is aged at least 2 years in charred oak barrels.
- Tennessee whiskey: Made only in Tennessee, this whiskey is filtered through sugar-maple charcoal and aged for 2 years in new charred barrels.

Brandy/cognac: Brandy is a distilled spirit made from the juice of fruit or grapes, and cognac is a type of brandy made from grapes grown under strict regulations in the Cognac region of France. Some common and unofficial brandy grades include:

- VS (very special): Aged at least $2\frac{1}{2}$ years in casks
- VSOP (very superior old pale): Aged a minimum of $4\frac{1}{2}$ years in casks.
- XO (extra old): Aged at least $6\frac{1}{2}$ years in casks.

Flavored liqueurs: These liqueurs are made by mixing or redistilling spirits over fruits or botanicals through infusion, percolation, or maceration. Some common favorites are:

- Amaretto
- Anisette
- Apricot
- Coffee
- Crème de cacao
- Crème de cassis
- Limoncello
- Maraschino
- Pomegranate
- Sloe gin
- Triple sec

Bitters: Bitters are modifiers generally made from alcohol, herbs, plants, or roots. A few drops add a great deal of flavor. The following varieties are commonly available:

- Peach
- Orange
- Blood orange
- Angostura
- Peychauds
- Mint
- Lemon
- Aged

WINES AND BEERS

Wines: Every bar should have a few bottles of the four primary varieties:

- White
- Red
- Port
- Sparkling/champagne

Beer: In order to satisfy a range of tastes, have on hand both an ale (smooth, light) and a lager (hearty, rich). The two primary types of beer are ale and lager.

- Ale is a sweet, full-bodied, and fruity beer made with top-fermenting yeast. Predominantly British and Belgian in origin. Stout is a dark ale made with roasted malt or barley that is usually fuller in flavor. Porter is sometimes used as an alternate name for stout, and it may indicate a stout that is stronger than usual. India pale ale (IPA) is a sparkling ale with a higher level of hops and a bitter flavor. Hefeweizen is an unfiltered wheat ale with a light, crisp, and fruity flavor. It is often served with a slice of lemon or orange to enhance its flavors.
- Lager is German and Czech in origin, with a wide range of flavors. Bock is a strong lager (originally from Einbeck, Germany) that may be dark, amber, or pale in color. Dopplebock is a Bavarian specialty beer that is very rich, with a malty flavor and a higher alcohol content. A pilsner is a pale lager with a light, clear-to-golden-yellow color and a distinct hoppy aroma and flavor.

Store-Bought Ingredients

Juice

- Cranberry
- Lemon
- Lime
- Grapefruit
- Orange
- Pineapple
- Tomato

Mixers

- Bottled water
- Club soda
- Cola and diet cola
- Ginger ale
- Grenadine
- Half & half
- Lemon-lime soda
- Tonic water

Standard Garnishes

- Maraschino and brandied cherries
- Spanish olives
- Lemons
- Limes
- Oranges
- Pearl onions

Homemade Ingredients

SYRUPS

Simple syrup: Simple syrup is used as a sweetening ingredient in many cocktails and is a combination of one part sugar to one part water. The basic recipe is:

Simple Syrup

1 cup super fine sugar
1 cup hot water

Stir or shake until sugar dissolves. Store in a sterile container in the refrigerator. Glass jars with lids are the preferred storage container; they are easily sterilized by filling them with boiling water.

Flavored syrups: Flavored syrups are easy to make and can enhance the classics with savory herbs and sweetness. Some syrups require adjusting the one-to-one ratio of sugar to water, but you can make almost any flavored syrup by adding your favorite flavor to the basic simple syrup recipe and following the directions below.

Brown Sugar Syrup

1 cup brown sugar

1 cup water

Cinnamon Syrup

1 cup super fine sugar

1 cup water

4 cinnamon sticks (or one heaping bar spoon of ground cinnamon)

Honey Syrup

1 cup honey

½ cup water

Honey Rosemary Syrup

1 cup honey

½ cup water

4 rosemary sprigs

Lavender Syrup

½ cup super fine sugar

¼ cup organic dried lavender

1 cup water

Lemon Grass Syrup

1 cup super fine sugar

1 cup water

1 lemon grass stalk (peeled and cut to fit into pan)

Vanilla Syrup

1 cup super fine sugar

1 cup water

1 vanilla bean (split in half)

Bring all ingredients to a boil on medium heat. Reduce heat and simmer for 8 to 10 minutes, until sugar is dissolved. Stir occasionally. Let cool. Use a sieve to strain the syrup into a sterilized and sealed container. Store in the refrigerator.

SOUR MIXERS

Fresh Sour

2 cups Fresh Lemon Juice (approximately 8 lemons juiced)

1 cup Simple Syrup (see page 24)

Stir well. Cover. Store in the refrigerator.

Fresh Limeade

2 cups Fresh Lime Juice (approximately 8 limes juiced)

1 cup Simple Syrup (see page 24)

Stir well. Cover. Store in the refrigerator.

Adds tartness when used as an alternative to lemonade.

PURÉES

All flavors of fruit or vegetable purée can be made by following these easy directions. For fruits, simply peel and cube them; for vegetables, cut and steam them. Add ingredients to a food processor or blender and blend until smooth. For additional sweetness, add Simple Syrup (see page 24) to taste. Strain through a sieve into a sealed container. Store in the refrigerator.

ORANGE OR LEMON SPIRALS

To make a simple and beautiful garnish, use a firm, room-temperature orange or lemon and a citrus peeler. Cut the top and bottom off the citrus fruit and insert the tip of the citrus peeler in to the pith of the fruit (the white area between the peel and pulp). Without moving the tool, slowly rotate the fruit around peeler until the tip is at the midway point. Repeat from the bottom. The fruit should be completely loosened from the skin. Make a diagonal cut in the peel and remove it. All fruit and pulp should be removed from the peel. Roll the peel tightly and place a toothpick through the center to hold it in place. Cut ¼-inch slices from the rolled-up fruit. Place spiral on cocktail by holding both ends of the spiral and gently twisting and spreading it open in one quick motion.

SPRING

Rebirth. Renewal. Anticipation.

SEASON'S BEST

Artichoke ‡ Asparagus ‡ Beets

Carrots ‡ Cucumbers ‡ Dandelion

Greens ‡ Fiddlehead Ferns ‡ Lettuce

Morels ‡ Papaya ‡ Pea Pods

Radishes ‡ Rhubarb ‡ Spinach

Strawberries ‡ Watercress ‡ Zucchini

Carrot Chic

A fresh welcome to spring.

1½ ounces carrot juice (about 2 medium carrots)
½ ounce Fresh Sour (see page 26)
1½ ounces orange vodka
½ ounce triple sec
Baby carrot (for garnish)

RIM INGREDIENTS
3 bar spoons super fine sugar
½ bar spoon ground ginger
Lime wedge

TO RIM THE GLASS: Measure sugar and ginger onto a small plate. Stir. Rim the outside top of glass with lime wedge. Roll the outside lip of glass in sugar mixture. Set aside.

Add carrot juice, Fresh Sour, orange vodka, and triple sec to mixing glass. Add ice to your tin. Shake well. Strain into cocktail glass.

Garnish with a baby carrot.

TOOL BOX

Mixing glass
Tin
Strainer
Bar spoon
Knife
Electric juicer
Cocktail glass

TOOL BOX

Mixing glass
Tin
Strainer
Muddler
Knife
Rocks glass

Cucumber Caipiroska

A refreshing spa experience in a glass.

4 lime wedges
1 ounce Simple Syrup (see page 24)
2 cucumber wheels (½-inch)
1½ ounces pear vodka

To a rocks glass, add lime wedges, Simple Syrup, cucumbers and vodka. Muddle until ingredients are well combined. Add ice to tin. Pour ingredients from rocks glass to mixing glass. Reserve the rocks glass. Shake well. Dump all ingredients from the shaker back into the seasoned rocks glass, and serve.

The Caipirinha and Caipiroska are the only classic cocktails muddled, shaken, and poured without straining into a serving glass. Made with a Brazilian rum called cachaca, which is made of 100 percent sugar cane, the Caipirinha was originally known as a "peasant drink" and is the national drink of Brazil. The Caipiroska is a vodka-based variation of the drink that is more popular among young Brazilian adults.

Rhubarb Strawberry Collins

A sweet and juicy addition to the classic Collins.

5 large, ripe strawberries
1 stalk of rhubarb
1½ ounces Fresh Sour (see page 26)
1½ ounces gin
Splash of pasteurized egg white (look for small cartons
   of pasteurized egg white in the dairy section)
Club soda

In electric juicer, juice 4 strawberries, set aside. Juice rhubarb into a separate glass. Set aside.

To mixing glass, add 1 ounce strawberry juice, 1½ ounces rhubarb juice, Fresh Sour, gin, and egg white. Add ice to tin and tall glass. Shake well. Strain into the iced-filled glass. Top with club soda.

Garnish with a strawberry heart by slicing the strawberry lengthwise into thin slices.

This drink dates from the late 1800s. Cocktail lore suggests this recipe is inspired by the Collins, which may have been invented in St. Louis or London. One story suggests that the original Tom Collins was made with "Old Tom" gin, a sweetened variety of gin that was available before London dry gin. When made with gin and Fresh Sour, the Collins is a true classic.

Spring Fresco

Perfect for an outdoor cocktail party.

10 tarragon leaves

4 thin radish slices

4 thin cucumber slices

½ ounce bianco vermouth

1 ounce grapefruit vodka

½ ounce Fresh Sour (see page 26)

½ ounce fresh orange juice

1 radish and tarragon sprig (for garnish)

In mixing glass, muddle tarragon, radish and cucumber slices, and vermouth. Add vodka, Fresh Sour, and orange juice. Add ice to tin. Shake well. Strain into cocktail glass.

Garnish with a radish wheel and tarragon sprig.

The Green Mule

A fresh twist on the classic Moscow Mule.

3 zucchini wheels
1 cucumber wheel
Juice of 1 lime wedge
2 ounces vodka
4 ounces ginger beer
Zucchini stick (for garnish)

In a rocks glass, muddle zucchini, cucumber, and juice squeezed from lime wedge. Add vodka. Fill glass with crushed ice and top with ginger beer. Stir well.

Garnish with a zucchini stick.

TOOL
BOX

Mixing glass

Tin

Strainer

Muddler

Bar spoon

Citrus press

Knife

Cocktail glass

Fresh Strawberry Daiquiri

A traditional Daiquiri with a kiss of spring.

2 sliced strawberries (optional)
½ ounce orange liqueur (optional)
1½ ounces white rum
1 bar spoon super fine sugar
Juice of ½ a pressed lime
Whole strawberry (for garnish)

RIM INGREDIENTS
4 bar spoons super fine sugar
Lime wedge

TO RIM THE GLASS: Measure sugar onto a small plate. Rim the outside top of glass with the lime wedge. Roll the outside lip of the glass in sugar. Set aside.

In mixing glass, muddle strawberry slices and orange liqueur, if using. Add rum, sugar, and lime. Add ice to tin. Shake well. Strain into sugar-rimmed glass.

Garnish with a strawberry.

The Daiquiri's main ingredients are rum, lime juice, and sugar. Jennings Cox, an American mining engineer working in Cuba for the Spanish American Iron Company, invented this drink in 1905 at the Venus Bar in Santiago, Cuba. It was a favorite of John F. Kennedy and Ernest Hemingway, who popularized the Daiquiri in the United States.

Spiced Beet Cocktail

A sophisticated, balanced blend of bold, spicy flavors.

- 1 beet (peeled and sliced)
- Juice of 3 pressed limes
- 2 bar spoons brown sugar
- Pinch of ground ginger
- 1½ ounces silver tequila
- ½ ounce mezcal
- 1 ounce Fresh Sour (see page 26)
- 1 beet leaf (for garnish)

To sauté pan, add sliced beet, lime juice, brown sugar, and ground ginger. Cover and simmer on medium heat for about 10 minutes, or until beets are tender. Stir occasionally. Remove beets. Let liquid cool.

To mixing glass, add silver tequila, mezcal, cooled beet liquid (about 2 ounces), and Fresh Sour. Add ice to tin. Shake well. Strain into cocktail glass.

Garnish with a beet leaf.

TOOL BOX

Sauté pan
Citrus press
Bar spoon
Mixing glass
Tin
Strainer
Knife
Cocktail glass

TOOL BOX

Mixing glass

Tin

Strainer

Muddler

Knife

Cocktail glass

Papaya Pisco Sour

Pairs wonderfully with Latin cuisine and spicy appetizers.

3 papaya cubes

Juice of 1 pressed lime

1 ounce Simple Syrup (see page 24)

2 ounces pisco brandy

Splash of pasteurized egg white (look for small cartons of
  pasteurized egg white in the dairy section)

Angostura bitters

In mixing glass, muddle papaya cubes and lime juice. Add
Simple Syrup, pisco brandy, and egg white. Add ice to tin.
Shake hard. Strain into cocktail glass.

Garnish with 3 drops Angostura bitters.

The Pisco Sour is the national drink of Chile and Peru, and which coun-
try the drink actually originated in is the subject of much dispute. Pisco
is a brandy made from the grapes grown in the wine-producing areas
of both countries.

Gingered Cherry Snap

Bright, tasty flavors liven up a spring afternoon.

- 3 pitted Bing cherries, sliced
- Juice from 1 lemon wedge
- ½ ounce ginger simple syrup
- ½ ounce sweet vermouth
- 1½ ounces dark rum
- Angostura bitters (for garnish)

In rocks glass, muddle cherries, lemon juice, and ginger simple syrup. Add vermouth and rum. Add ice to glass. Stir well.

Garnish with 3 drops Angostura bitters.

TOOL BOX

Muddler
Bar spoon
Rocks glass

TOASTS FOR
SPRING

Happiness is like a kiss,
It feels better when you give it to someone else.

To each, to all, happiness, health,
And fortunes grown tall.

May we be happy and our enemies know it.

Here's to happy times,
May they come often and stay long!

SUMMER

Blossoming. Fresh. Inspirational.

SEASON'S BEST

Apricots ‡ Bell Peppers ‡ Blackberries

Blueberries ‡ Cantaloupe ‡ Celery

Cherries ‡ Chick Peas ‡ Clams

Cucumber ‡ Currants ‡ Figs

Gooseberries ‡ Grapes ‡ Honeydew

Lime ‡ Lychee Nuts ‡ Mango

Nectarines ‡ Peaches ‡ Plums

Raspberries ‡ Tomatoes ‡ Watermelon

Zucchini

TOOL
BOX

Watermelon Margarita

Brings together cocktail and picnic traditions.

4 watermelon cubes (1-inch) (seeds removed)
Juice of ½ a pressed lime
1½ ounces Fresh Sour (see page 26)
1½ ounces silver tequila
½ ounce triple sec
Watermelon wedge (for garnish)

RIM INGREDIENTS
4 bar spoons super fine sugar
1 bar spoon sea salt
1 bar spoon pink peppercorns (crushed)
Lime wedge

Mixing glass
Tin
Strainer
Knife
Muddler
Bar spoon
Citrus press
Cocktail glass

TO RIM THE GLASS: On a small plate, measure sugar, sea salt, and crushed pink peppercorns. Stir gently. Rim the outside top of the glass with a lime wedge. Roll the outside lip of the glass in the sugar mixture. Set aside.

In mixing glass, muddle watermelon cubes and lime juice. Add Fresh Sour, tequila, and triple sec. Add ice to tin. Shake all ingredients well. Strain into rimmed cocktail glass.

Garnish with a watermelon wedge.

CONTINUED ON NEXT PAGE

CONTINUED FROM PREVIOUS PAGE

The Margarita is surrounded by many stories, and no one is certain who created this cocktail. Credit could go to a Mexico City socialite named Margarita, who charged her bartender with making a signature cocktail appropriate for her many parties. Another bit of lore surrounding this blend of tequila and triple sec names Pancho Morales of Tommy's Place in Juarez, Mexico, as the drink's creator. According to that story, a woman ordered a Magnolia cocktail, which is made with brandy, triple sec, and champagne. Pancho could not recall the Magnolia's ingredients, so he improvised, and the Margarita was born. Whichever story is true, one thing is for sure—the Margarita is America's best-selling cocktail.

Breakfast Cocktail

A favorite addition to any brunch.

2 ounces fresh apricot juice
1 ounce fresh orange juice
2 ounces orange vodka
½ ounce pink grapefruit juice
Apricot slice (for garnish)

In an electric juicer, separately juice 1 ripe apricot and then 1 orange. Add orange vodka, apricot juice, orange juice, and pink grapefruit juice to mixing glass. Add ice to tin. Shake well. Add crushed ice to tall glass. Strain cocktail into glass.

Garnish with an apricot slice.

TIP: Omit the vodka to make a delicious alcohol-free version.

TOOL BOX

Mixing glass
Tin
Strainer
Knife
Electric juicer
Tall/Collins glass

TOOL BOX

Muddler
Bar spoon
Citrus press
Knife
Straws
Cocktail pick
Tall/Collins glass

Blueberry Lavender Mojito

Lusciously aromatic with bursts of flavor. Made to be sipped and savored.

> 10–15 mint leaves
> 1 ounce Lavender Syrup (see page 25) or Simple Syrup (see page 24)
> Juice of ½ a pressed lime
> 15–20 blueberries
> 1½ ounces white rum
> Club soda

In tall glass, muddle mint leaves, Lavender Syrup, lime juice, 15 blueberries, and rum. Muddle just enough to combine flavors, being careful not to over-muddle. Fill glass with crushed ice. Top with club soda. Stir with bar spoon until well blended.

To garnish, place 3 to 4 blueberries on a cocktail pick. Serve with a straw.

This drink dates from the early 1900s. The Mojito was created at the La Bodeguita del Medio Bar in Cuba. Ernest Hemingway made this cocktail an international sensation in the 1940s.

**TOOL
BOX**

Muddler
Knife
Bar spoon
Rocks glass

Peach Julep

This julep is a sure bet on Derby Day.

10-15 mint leaves
1 ounce Brown Sugar Syrup (see page 25)
3 fresh peach slices
2 ounces Kentucky straight bourbon whiskey
Mint sprig (for garnish)

To a rocks glass, add mint, Brown Sugar Syrup, and peaches. Muddle until well combined. Add whiskey. Fill glass with crushed ice. Stir.

Garnish with a mint sprig.

Although the Julep was created in the early 1700s, it first appeared in print in an 1803 book published in London by John Davis. Traditionally served in silver or pewter cups and held only by the bottom and top edges of the cup, the Julep did not become the signature cocktail of Churchill Downs until 1938.

Blackberry Cinnamon Mojito

Contemporary flavors spice up the traditional Mojito.
Serve with your favorite barbecue.

TOOL BOX

Muddler
Bar spoon
Citrus press
Knife
Tall/Collins glass

10-15 mint leaves
1 ounce Cinnamon Syrup (see page 25) or Simple Syrup
   (see page 24)
Juice of ½ a pressed lime
8 blackberries
1½ ounces aged rum
Club soda
1 mint sprig and remaining blackberry (for garnish)

In tall glass, muddle mint, Cinnamon Syrup, lime
juice, 7 blackberries, and rum. Muddle just enough to
combine flavors, being careful not to over-muddle. Fill
glass with crushed ice. Top with club soda. Stir with
bar spoon until well blended.

To garnish, spear a blackberry with a mint sprig.

Raspberry French 75

Toast your special occasion with a savory celebration cocktail.

4 sage leaves

5 fresh raspberries

1½ ounces Fresh Sour (see page 26)

1½ ounces gin

Splash of champagne or sparkling wine

1 sage sprig (for garnish)

In mixing glass, muddle sage leaves, 4 raspberries, and Fresh Sour. Add gin. Add ice to tin. Shake well. Add a splash of champagne to ingredients in shaker. Gently rock all ingredients. Strain into champagne glass.

Garnish with a sage sprig gently speared through remaining raspberry.

The French 75 was created by Raoul Lufbery, a pilot in the Escadrille Americaine air fighting unit. The cocktail was originally blended with cognac and champagne and was named after a type of French artillery used in World War I because it was said to strike just as hard.

Mixing glass

Tin

Strainer

Muddler

Champagne flute

TOOL BOX

Muddler
Knife
Bar spoon
Tall/Collins glass

Gooseberry Lemonade

Summer citrus with tart sweetness. Perfect for outdoor entertaining.

 4 gooseberries (sliced in half)
 Splash of Simple Syrup (see page 24)
 2 ounces chardonnay
 4 ounces pink lemonade
 Gooseberry (for garnish)

In tall glass, muddle gooseberries and Simple Syrup. Fill glass with crushed ice. Add chardonnay and pink lemonade. Stir until well combined.

Garnish with a gooseberry placed on the lip of the glass.

**TOOL
BOX**

Mixing glass

Tin

Strainer

Knife

Muddler

Tall/Collins
glass

Plum Sour

Simple ingredients with bold, balanced flavors.

> 3 plum wedges
>
> 2 ounces Fresh Sour (see page 26)
>
> 2 ounces bourbon
>
> Splash of pasteurized egg white (look for small cartons
> of pasteurized egg white in the dairy section)
>
> Peach bitters

In a mixing glass, muddle plums, Fresh Sour, and
bourbon until well combined. Add egg white. Add
crushed ice to tall glass. Set aside. Add ice to tin and
shake cocktail. Strain over crushed ice into tall glass.
Top with 3 drops of peach bitters.

In his 1862 book *How to Mix Drinks*, Jerry Thomas describes sours
as drinks made with brandy. Today, a sour is a mixed drink with a
base spirit, lemon or lime juice, and a sweetener.

TOOL BOX

Mixing glass
Tin
Strainer
Sieve
Knife
Muddler
Cocktail glass

Fresh Tomato Bloody Mary

Ripe summer flavors. Not just for brunch anymore!

6 cherry tomatoes
1 basil leaf
Pinch of fresh oregano
Pinch of salt
Pinch of ground black pepper
Dash of Tabasco sauce
Dash of Worcestershire sauce
Juice of 1 lemon wedge
1½ ounces citrus vodka (may substitute silver tequila)
1 oregano sprig (for garnish)

In mixing glass, muddle 5 tomatoes, basil, oregano, salt, black pepper, Tabasco sauce, Worcestershire sauce, and lemon juice. Add citrus vodka. Add ice to tin. Shake well. Double-strain into cocktail glass using the strainer on the shaker while pouring contents through the sieve placed over the glass.

Garnish with an oregano sprig speared through remaining cherry tomato.

The Bloody Mary was created in the 1920s by Fernand "Pete" Petiot, a bartender at Harry's New York Bar in Paris, France. The name stuck because it reminded a patron of a woman named Mary from The Bucket of Blood Club in Chicago. In the 1930s, Petiot unsuccessfully tried to change the name of this famous cocktail to the Red Snapper.

TOOL BOX

Blender
Cocktail pick
Straw
Tall/Collins
glass

Lychee Madras

Crisp citrus with a nutty sweetness.

1½ ounces lemon vodka
2 ounces cranberry juice
1 ounce fresh orange juice
Juice of 1 lime wedge
3 lychee nuts

Place 1 tall glass of ice in blender. Add vodka, cranberry juice, orange juice, lime juice, and 2 lychee nuts. Blend until ice is crushed. Pour into a tall glass.

Garnish with remaining lychee nut on a cocktail pick.

Caliente Mango Freeze

Kick up your party with this hot and cool cocktail.
Serve with chips and salsa.

1 mango (cubed)
1 jalapeño pepper (cut into wheels)
¼ cup Simple Syrup (see page 24)
2 scoops lemon sorbet
½ ounce Fresh Sour (see page 26)
2 ounces reposado tequila
Lime zest

Add mango cubes and jalapeño wheels to sauté pan
with Simple Syrup. Sauté on medium heat until
mango is soft. Cool.

Add lemon sorbet to rocks glass. In mixing glass,
muddle mango compote, Fresh Sour, and tequila. Add
ice to tin. Shake well. Strain over sorbet. Zest about ¼
teaspoon of lime over cocktail. Enjoy with a spoon and
straw.

**TOOL
BOX**

Mixing glass
Tin
Strainer
Knife
Muddler
Ice cream scoop
Grater
Sauté pan
Rocks glass

TOOL BOX

Mixing glass

Tin

Strainer

Knife

Muddler

Citrus press

Cocktail glass

Honeydew Sake Cocktail

Elevate the subtle flavors of honeydew with lemon grass and sake. Serve with Asian cuisine.

> Juice of 1 medium lemon (approximately 1½ ounces)
> 5 1-inch honeydew cubes
> 2 ounces sake
> ½ ounce Lemon Grass Syrup (see page 25)
> Small stalk of lemon grass (for garnish)

To mixing glass, add lemon juice and 4 honeydew cubes. Muddle. Add sake and Lemon Grass Syrup. Add ice to tin. Shake well. Strain into cocktail glass.

Garnish with remaining honeydew cube speared with a stalk of lemon grass.

Cantaloupe Cobbler

Subtle and delicious.

5 1-inch cantaloupe cubes
2 1-inch pineapple cubes
2 fresh pitted cherries
1 ounce fresh lemon juice
1 ounce Simple Syrup (see page 24)
½ ounce orange liqueur
1½ ounces bourbon

In a mixing glass, muddle 4 cantaloupe cubes, 1 pineapple cube, and cherry. Add lemon juice, simple syrup, orange liqueur, and bourbon. Add ice to tin. Shake well. Strain into a crushed-ice-filled rocks glass.

Garnish with remaining cantaloupe and pineapple cubes and cherry.

**TOOL
BOX**

Muddler
Tin
Strainer
Mixing glass
Rocks glass

TOOL BOX

Blender
Tall/Collins
glass

Apricot Lemonade Freeze

Chilly and delightful on a hot summer day.

2 very ripe apricot cubes (1-inch)
2 ounces fresh lemon juice
½ ounce Simple Syrup (see page 24)
1½ ounces apricot brandy
¼ ounce amaretto
Lemon wheel (for garnish)

In a blender, combine all ingredients except amaretto and lemon wheel. Blend until smooth. Pour into glass and float amaretto on top of the cocktail.

Garnish with lemon wheel and serve with a straw.

TOASTS FOR
SUMMER

I thank you for your welcome,
Which was cordial,
And your cordial,
Which is welcome.

Nothing but the best for our hostess,
That's why she has us as friends.

May the luck of the Irish possess you,
May the devil fly off with your worries,
And may God bless you forever and ever.
—Irish folklore

AUTUMN

Abundance. Harvest. Appreciation.

SEASON'S BEST

Apples ‡ Celery Root ‡ Chestnuts

Coconut ‡ Cranberry ‡ Dates ‡ Fennel

Figs ‡ Grapes ‡ Kumquats ‡ Leeks

Onions ‡ Papaya ‡ Pear ‡ Persimmons

Pomegranate ‡ Pumpkin ‡ Quince

Butternut Squash ‡ White Truffles

Walnuts

Cozy Pomegranate Cider

Warm up to these rich, fall flavors.

2 cups apple cider
1 cup red wine
½ cup pomegranate juice
2 cinnamon sticks
10–15 whole cloves
4–5 pomegranate seeds (per cocktail, for garnish)

RIM INGREDIENTS
4 bar spoons super fine sugar
¼ bar spoon cinnamon
Lime wedge

TO RIM THE GLASS: On a small plate, measure sugar
and cinnamon. Stir. Rim the outside top of mug with
lime wedge. Roll the outside rim of mug in the sugar
mixture. Set aside.

Add apple cider, wine, pomegranate juice, cinnamon
sticks, and cloves to a saucepan. Bring to a simmer on
low heat. Strain hot cider through a sieve into sugar-
rimmed mug.

Garnish by dropping pomegranate seeds in cider.
Seeds will gently float to the bottom of the glass.

TOOL BOX

Sauce pan
Knife
Bar spoon
Ladle
Sieve
Coffee mug

TOOL BOX

Mixing glass

Tin

Strainer

Cocktail pick

Cocktail glass

Gibson with Homemade Cocktail Onions

Homemade cocktail onions are perfect in a Martini and make a wonderful hostess gift.

> Dry vermouth
>
> 3 ounces gin
>
> 2 Homemade Cocktail Onions (see recipe on next page) (for garnish)

Rinse the inside of cocktail glass with dry vermouth by swirling vermouth on inside of glass and pouring it out, leaving only residue in the glass. Add gin to mixing glass. Add ice to tin. Shake well. Strain into seasoned cocktail glass.

Garnish with 2 Homemade Cocktail Onions on a pick.

The Gibson cocktail is named after an American diplomat who served in Europe during Prohibition. He was described as a teeto-taller who attended many events where Martinis were served. To avoid drinking, he requested that his glass of water be garnished with an onion, so he could easily distinguish it from the other cocktails.

Homemade Cocktail Onion Recipe

1 pound fresh pearl onions
½ cup cider vinegar
½ cup red wine vinegar
½ cup water
½ cup salt
⅔ cup sugar
1 rosemary sprig
8 juniper berries
12 whole allspice
1 bar spoon chai spice blend
1 bar spoon black pepper
½ bar spoon minced garlic
1 cup bianco vermouth

To a saucepan, add pearl onions and cover with water. Bring to a boil on high heat. Reduce heat and simmer for 10 minutes. Drain water. Cut ends off onions and peel. Place onions in a glass container.

Add following ingredients back to the saucepan: cider vinegar, red wine vinegar, water, salt, sugar, rosemary, juniper berries, allspice, chai spice blend, black pepper, and minced garlic. Let ingredients simmer on low heat for 20 minutes. Strain liquid over onions. Let cool. Add bianco vermouth. Mix together.

Store onions and liquid in a sealed container in refrigerator.

TOOL
BOX

Apple corer
Mixing glass
Tin
Strainer
Knife
Muddler
Cored apple

The Apple Cocktail

Dazzle your guests with this Thanksgiving cocktail. Served in an apple instead of a glass.

> 1 whole apple (select one with a flatter bottom)
> Juice of 1 lemon wedge
> 1 apple wedge (cut in half)
> 1 ounce unsweetened apple juice
> 1 ounce limoncello
> ½ ounce vanilla vodka
> Splash cranberry juice
> 1 cinnamon stick (for garnish)

Core the apple to about the halfway point. Be certain not to cut through the bottom. Use the lemon wedge to squeeze a small amount of lemon juice on inside of cored apple. Set aside.

In mixing glass, muddle apple wedge and unsweetened apple juice. Add limoncello, vanilla vodka, and cranberry juice. Shake well. Strain into cored apple and serve with a small straw.

Garnish with a cinnamon stick.

Cinnamon Fig Sidecar

Enjoy the rich, toasty flavors of cognac as it brings out the sweetness of fresh figs.

1 black mission fig
1½ ounces Fresh Sour (see page 24)
Pinch of cinnamon
½ ounce orange curaçao
1½ ounces VSOP cognac

RIM INGREDIENTS
4 bar spoons super fine sugar
Lime wedge

TO RIM THE GLASS: On a small plate, measure the sugar. Rim the outside top of glass with lime wedge. Roll the outside rim of the glass in the sugar. Set aside.

Remove stem from the fig, cut a thin slice for the garnish, and dice the remainder. Add diced fig and Fresh Sour to mixing glass. Muddle until well combined. Add a small pinch of cinnamon, orange curaçao, and cognac. Add ice to tin. Shake hard. Strain into sugar-rimmed cocktail glass. Garnish with fig slice.

This cocktail was created at Paris's Harry's New York Bar by barman Pete Petiot. It was named in honor of a World War I American Army captain living in Paris who was driven to the bar each day in a motor-cycle sidecar. The original Sidecar is a fine blend of brandy, triple sec, and lemon.

Piña Colada Cocktail

Bring a touch of summer to autumn.

1½ ounces coconut rum
2 ounces fresh coconut water
½ ounce fresh pineapple juice
Juice of ½ a pressed lime
Pineapple leaf (for garnish)

RIM INGREDIENTS
2 bar spoons honey
4 bar spoons coconut flakes

TO RIM THE GLASS: Measure honey onto a small plate. Measure coconut flakes onto a different small plate. First, rotate the rim of the glass in the honey, coating the top outer lip. Next, roll the honey rim in the coconut until it is evenly coated. Set aside.

To mixing glass, add coconut rum, coconut water, pineapple juice, and lime juice. Add ice to tin. Shake well. Strain into coconut-rimmed cocktail glass.

Garnish with a pineapple leaf.

The Piña Colada was first introduced in 1954 by bartender Ramon "Monchito" Marrero at the Caribe Hilton Hotel in Puerto Rico. It is the official beverage of the hotel. There is also a bar in old San Juan that makes a similar claim.

TOOL BOX

Mixing glass
Tin
Strainer
Citrus press
Bar spoon
Cocktail glass

Grape Escape

A playful cocktail reminiscent of grape soda.

9 concord grapes
½ ounce concord grape juice
½ ounce peach schnapps
1 ounce currant vodka
1 ounce Fresh Sour (see page 24)
Club soda
2 frozen concord grapes (for garnish)

In mixing glass, muddle grapes and grape juice. Add peach schnapps, vodka, and Fresh Sour. Add ice to tin. Shake well. Strain into cocktail glass. Top with club soda.

Garnish with 2 frozen concord grapes on a pick.

TOOL BOX

Mixing glass

Tin

Strainer

Muddler

Cocktail pick

Cocktail glass

Pear Essence Cosmopolitan

Autumn's best inspires new tradition in this classic favorite.

2 d'Anjou pear slices
Juice of ½ a pressed lime
1 ounce cranberry juice
1½ ounces citrus vodka
½ ounce triple sec
3 cranberries (for garnish)

In mixing glass, muddle pear slices, lime juice, and cranberry juice. Add vodka and triple sec. Add ice to tin. Shake well. Double-strain into glass, using the strainer over the shaker while pouring contents through a sieve placed over the glass.

Garnish with 3 cranberries on a cocktail pick.

The Cosmopolitan got its start between 1956 and 1970, when Ocean Spray began to include cocktail recipes on the label of its fruit juice containers. The original version, known as the Harpoon, was made with vodka, cranberry juice, and lime. Later, triple sec was added and the drink was newly dubbed the Cosmopolitan. The drink was popularized in the 1990s by the television series *Sex and the City*.

TOOL BOX

Mixing glass

Tin

Strainer

Knife

Muddler

Tall/Collins glass

Refrescante Fennel Cocktail

A great complement to savory or spicy food.

Juice of 1 lime wedge

10 fennel seeds

2 ounces añejo tequila

3 ounces fresh orange juice

Lime wheel (for garnish)

In mixing glass, squeeze juice from lime wedge over fennel seeds and muddle. Add tequila and fresh orange juice. Add ice to tin. Shake well. Fill tall glass with crushed ice. Strain cocktail into glass.

Garnish with a lime wheel.

Persimmon Indian Summer

A perfect treat after raking leaves or enjoying the crisp autumn air.

    4 persimmons (cubed)
    1 ounce Fresh Sour (see page 24)
    ½ ounce pomegranate juice
    6 whole cloves
    1½ ounces brandy
    Orange wedge (for garnish)

In mixing glass, muddle persimmon cubes and Fresh Sour. Add pomegranate juice, 3 cloves, and brandy. Add ice to tin. Shake well. Double-strain into glass using the strainer on the shaker while pouring contents through a sieve placed over the glass.

Garnish with an orange wedge decorated with remaining cloves.

TOOL BOX

Mixing glass
Tin
Strainer
Knife
Muddler
Cocktail glass

Pumpkin Cocktail

Add this to your Halloween or Thanksgiving dessert menu.

1½ ounces pumpkin liqueur
1 ounce orange vodka
½ ounce half & half
Splash of Vanilla Syrup (see page 26)
Gooseberry (for garnish)

RIM INGREDIENTS
4 bar spoons super fine sugar
¼ bar spoon ground cinnamon
Lime wedge

TO RIM THE GLASS: Measure sugar and cinnamon onto a small plate. Rim outside top of glass with lime wedge. Roll the outside rim of glass in sugar mixture. Set aside.

Add pumpkin liqueur, orange vodka, half and half, and Vanilla Syrup to mixing glass. Add ice to tin. Shake well. Strain into cocktail glass.

Garnish with a gooseberry. Peel back the outer leaves of the berry. Slit the bottom of the berry. Rest on the rim of the glass.

TOOL BOX

Mixing glass
Tin
Strainer
Bar spoon
Knife
Cocktail glass

TOOL BOX

Bar spoon

Tall/Collins glass

Amante Guava

Sweet and delicious.

2 ounces guava juice

1 ounce lime juice

½ ounce agave nectar

2 ounces reposado tequila

Orange bitters (for garnish)

Lime wheel (for garnish)

Add guava juice, lime juice, agave nectar, and tequila to a tall, ice-filled glass. Stir.

Garnish with 3 to 5 shakes of orange bitters and lime wheel.

TOASTS FOR
AUTUMN

Here's to our guest—
Don't let him rest.
But keep his elbow bending.
'Tis time to drink—
Full time to think
Tomorrow—when you're mending.

All our guests make us happy,
Some by coming, and others by going.

The ornament of a house
is the guests who frequent it.

WINTER

Cozy. Blustery. Reflection.

SEASON'S BEST

Avocado ‡ Bananas ‡ Black Truffles

Blood Oranges ‡ Caviar ‡ Celery Root

Chestnuts ‡ Grapefruit ‡ Jicama

Kiwi ‡ Kumquats ‡ Lemons ‡ Oranges

Parsnips ‡ Passion Fruit ‡ Pineapple

Tangerines

Caviar Martini

Luxury in every sip.

> Splash dry vermouth
> 3 ounces gin
> Caviar (for garnish)

Rinse the inside of cocktail glass with vermouth by swirling vermouth on the inside of the glass and pouring it out, leaving only residue in the glass. Add gin to mixing glass and ice to tin. Shake well. Strain into seasoned cocktail glass.

Garnish with caviar on a fancy spoon.

There are many stories surrounding the history of the Martini. The most well-known is that the Martini is a version of the original cocktail known as the Martinez, which consisted of a sweeter gin called "Old Tom," maraschino cherry liqueur, and bitters. The Martinez was served with a lemon twist. This cocktail was named for a customer who drank at the Occidental Hotel in San Francisco every morning before boarding a ferry to Martinez, California. Today's Martinis consist of gin and dry vermouth garnished with an olive, onion, or lemon twist.

TOOL BOX

Mixing glass

Tin

Strainer

Mother-of-pearl or other fancy spoon

Cocktail glass

TOOL BOX

Mixing glass
Tin
Strainer
Cocktail glass

1862

Serve before any meal as an aperitif.

1¼ ounce bianco vermouth
¾ ounce orange curaçao
Juice of 1 lemon wedge
¾ ounce Passion Fruit Purée (see page 27)
Splash of spumante sparkling wine
Orange and lemon spirals (see page 27) (for garnish)

To mixing glass, add vermouth, orange curaçao, lemon juice, and Passion Fruit Purée. Add ice to tin. Shake well. Add spumante. Rock contents of shaker gently. Strain into cocktail glass.

Garnish with an orange and lemon spiral.

As a member of the United States Bartenders Guild, Bridget competed in the Bacardi Martini Grand Prix, the most prestigious cocktail competition in the world. Her 1862 took home the silver medal.

Hot Banana Buttered Rum

Warm the hearts of your guests with these smells and tastes of the holidays.

1 pound unsalted sweet cream butter
   (room temperature)
1½ bar spoons ground cinnamon
1½ bar spoons Jamaican allspice
5 bar spoons super fine sugar
10-12 whole cloves
3 medium bananas (optional)
1½ ounces aged or spiced rum
Cinnamon stick (for garnish)

Using a spoon, mix butter, cinnamon, allspice, sugar, and cloves together until well combined. Cool in refrigerator for 2 hours.

BANANA VERSION: Slice bananas into 1-inch slices. Add bananas and 5 heaping bar spoons of butter mixture to sauté pan. Sauté until bananas are soft. Add back to bowl of butter mixture. Stir well. Cool as directed.

SPIRIT-FREE VERSION: Hold the rum.

To a coffee mug, add 2 heaping bar spoons of butter mixture. Add 1½ ounces of aged rum. Fill mug with hot water. Stir until butter is melted.

Garnish with a cinnamon stick.

TOOL BOX

Spoon
Sauté pan
Bar spoon
Knife
Large mixing bowl
Coffee mug

TOOL BOX

Mixing glass

Tin

Knife

Muddler

Strainer or
small sieve

Bar spoon

Cocktail glass

Savory Avocado Cocktail

The avocado adds a creamy twist to the Margarita.
Excellent with Mexican and spicy food.

1 whole avocado
5 fresh tarragon leaves
1½ ounces Fresh Sour (see page 26)
Juice of ½ a pressed lime
1½ ounces añejo tequila
½ ounce triple sec
Tarragon sprig (for garnish)

RIM INGREDIENTS
4 bar spoons super fine sugar
1½ bar spoons sea salt
Lime wedge

TO RIM THE GLASS: On a small plate, mix sugar and
salt. Rim the outside top of glass with lime wedge. Roll
the outside rim of glass in sugar mixture. Set aside.

Peel and cut avocado into 1-inch cubes. To mixing
glass, add 1 cube of avocado, 5 tarragon leaves, Fresh
Sour, and lime. Muddle until avocado is well mixed.
Add tequila and triple sec. Add ice to the tin. Shake all
ingredients well. Double-strain into glass, using the
strainer on the shaker while pouring contents through
a sieve over the glass.

Garnish with a tarragon sprig.

TOOL BOX

Mixing glass
Tin
Strainer
Cocktail glass

Mary Pickford

Tropical flavors come to life with the fruit of the season.

1½ ounces white rum
½ ounce maraschino liqueur
¼ ounce grenadine
2 ounces fresh pineapple juice
Pineapple spear (for garnish)

To mixing glass, add rum, maraschino liqueur, grenadine, and pineapple juice. Add ice to tin. Shake well. Strain into cocktail glass.

Garnish with a pineapple spear.

This cocktail was created in 1920 at the Hotel Nacional de Cuba, Havana. This refreshing cocktail uses native Cuban ingredients and was named after Mary Pickford, the popular star of silent films who was also known as "America's Sweetheart" and "Little Mary."

Muddler
Bar spoon
Knife
Rocks glass

Tangerine Orange Mule

Bright citrus flavors make this a modern cocktail.

3 tangerine segments (peeled)
Juice of 1 lime wedge
1½ ounces orange vodka
Splash of ginger beer
Lime wheel (for garnish)

In a rocks glass, muddle tangerine segments and lime juice. Add orange vodka. Fill glass with crushed ice. Top with ginger beer. Stir with bar spoon until well combined.

Garnish with a lime wheel.

The name Moscow Mule refers to the taste of vodka with an added "kick" provided by the rich flavors of ginger beer. The Moscow Mule was a marriage of interests and combined effort of Jack Morgan, the owner of the Cock 'n' Bull Tavern and a producer of ginger beer; John Martin, the president of a spirits company; and Rudolph Kunett, who worked for a division of that same company. The drink was traditionally served in a copper mug.

Kiwi Champagne

A perfect toast to the holidays.

TOOL
BOX

Knife
Mixing glass
Tin
Strainer
Muddler
Champagne
flute

4 slices of peeled kiwi fruit
Juice of 1 lime wedge
1 sugar cube
4 ounces prosecco sparkling wine
Orange bitters

In mixing glass, muddle kiwi, lime juice, and sugar cube. Add prosecco. Add ice to tin. Rock contents of shaker gently. Strain into flute. Shake 2 drops of orange bitters on top of cocktail.

TOOL BOX

Bar spoon
Muddler
Knife
Rocks glass

Red Grapefruit Brown Derby

This herbaceous, sweet version of the Brown Derby is meant to be sipped slowly and enjoyed with friends.

> 4 small red grapefruit wedges (peel removed)
> 1 ounce Honey Rosemary Syrup (see page 25)
> 2 ounces rye whiskey
> 1 rosemary sprig (for garnish)

In a rocks glass, muddle grapefruit and Honey Rosemary Syrup until well combined. Add rye whiskey. Fill to the top with crushed ice. Stir with bar spoon.

Garnish with rosemary sprig.

The Brown Derby was created in the 1930s at California's Vendome Club and named in honor of Wilshire Boulevard's Brown Derby restaurant.

Tall Meyer Lemon Southside

A friendly crowd pleaser, just right for entertaining.

TOOL BOX

Mixing glass

Tin

Strainer

Citrus press

Knife

Tall/Collins glass

- 2 ounces gin
- 2 ounces juice of Meyer lemons (approximately 2 lemons)
- 1 ounce Honey Syrup (see page 25)
- 10 mint leaves
- Splash of pasteurized egg white (optional) (look for small cartons of pasteurized egg white in the dairy section)
- Club soda
- Lemon wheel (for garnish)

To mixing glass, add gin, lemon juice, Honey Syrup, mint leaves, and egg white, if using. Add ice to tin and to tall glass. Set glass aside. Shake well. Strain into tall glass. Top with club soda.

Garnish with lemon wheel.

Although the Southside has a few stories surrounding its origin, one classic favorite is that it was developed during Prohibition by a south-side Chicago gang leader who used sugar and lemon to mask the flavor of bootleg gin. The 21 Club in New York also claims that it is the home of this deliciously refreshing cocktail.

TOOL BOX

Mixing glass

Tin

Strainer

Citrus press

Tall/Collins glass

Blood Orange Rickey

As crisp and colorful as a winter sunset.

> 1½ ounces gin
> Juice of 1 pressed blood orange (approximately 2 ounces)
> Juice of ½ a pressed lime
> Club soda
> Blood orange slice (for garnish)

To mixing glass, add gin, blood orange juice, and lime juice. Add ice to tin. Shake well. Strain into ice-filled tall glass. Top with club soda.

Garnish with a blood orange slice.

On an extremely hot, muggy day in 1890, a barman at the Washington, DC bar Shoemaker's made a new drink by simply squeezing lime into a glass of gin and adding soda from a siphon. Colonel Rickey, an English officer and lobbyist, was the first patron to try it; he enjoyed it so much, he asked for seconds. The barman named the drink the Gin Rickey, and its ingredients remain gin, fresh lime, and soda to this day.

Jam Thyme Fizz

Bubbly and bursting with rhubarb flavor.

1 bar spoon rhubarb jam
½ ounce Cinnamon Syrup (see page 25)
½ ounce fresh lime juice
1 ounce VSOP cognac
2 ounces prosecco sparkling wine
Sprig thyme (for garnish)

To mixing glass, add jam, Cinnamon Syrup, lime juice, and cognac. Add ice to tin. Shake well. Strain into champagne flute. Top with prosecco.

Garnish with a thyme sprig.

TOOL BOX

Bar spoon
Mixing glass
Tin
Strainer
Champagne flute

TOASTS FOR
WINTER

May you have the hindsight to know where you've been,
The foresight to know where you're going,
And the insight to know when you're going too far.

May you look back on the past with as much
Pleasure as you look forward to the future.

May we all be alive this time in twelve months.

To champagne,
The drink that makes you see double,
And feel single.

INFUSIONS

Infusions marry your favorite spirit with a season's freshest fruits, produce, herbs, and spices. The combinations are limitless since infusions can be enjoyed just as they are, or used as the base spirit in a creative cocktail, this chapter includes flavorful combinations and cocktail recipes for each infusion.

Making Your Infusion

Each market-fresh infusion recipe should be made in a 3-quart jar. Remember, the container must be washed and rinsed well, have a lid, and, most importantly, be made of glass. Never attempt to make an infusion in a plastic bottle.

Depending on the ripeness of the fruit, each recipe might produce a larger quantity than can fit back into the original liquor bottle. It's a good idea to have additional clean bottles on hand to accommodate any extra amounts. Always choose the freshest produce, and wash it thoroughly. Always plan ahead: Some infusions can take up to 2 weeks to be ready. As you will find, they are worth the wait.

SPRING INFUSIONS

Strawberry–Rosemary Infusion

Flavors of the vine right into your glass.

- 10 pints of sliced strawberries
- 7 rosemary sprigs
- 2 750 ml gin

Place strawberries and rosemary in 3-quart glass infusion jar. Pour gin over the fruit. Save original gin bottles. Let rest for 7 days at room temperature. Using a funnel and sieve, strain liquid back into empty liquor bottles. Refrigerate.

Red Martini

3 ounces Strawberry–Rosemary Infusion

Dash of Simple Syrup (see page 24)

Add Strawberry–Rosemary Infusion to mixing glass. Add Simple Syrup to taste. Add ice to tin. Shake well. Strain into a cocktail glass. Garnish with a rosemary sprig.

Salty Puppy Cocktail

2 ounces Strawberry–Rosemary Infusion

3 ounces pink grapefruit juice

RIM INGREDIENTS

Lime wedge

2 bar spoons sea salt

TO RIM THE GLASS: Measure salt onto a small plate. Rim the outside top of the glass with a lime wedge. Roll the outside rim of the glass in the salt. Set aside.

Add ice to a rocks glass. Pour in Strawberry–Rosemary Infusion and pink grapefruit juice. Stir.

Cucumber–Papaya Infusion

Crisp refreshment on a hot summer day.

5 English cucumbers (thinly sliced)

2 whole papayas (peeled and cubed)

2 750 ml gin

Layer fruit into 3-quart glass infusion jar. Add gin. Save liquor bottles. Let rest for 7 days at room temperature. Using a funnel and sieve, strain liquid back into bottles. Refrigerate.

Spa Cocktail

3 ounces Cucumber–Papaya Infusion

½ ounce Fresh Sour (see page 26)

Cucumber slice (for garnish)

To mixing glass, add Cucumber–Papaya Infusion and Fresh Sour. Add ice to tin. Shake well. Strain into a cocktail glass.

Garnish with a cucumber slice.

Tea for Two Cocktail

This cocktail is made in a pitcher and meant to be shared.

6 ounces Cucumber–Papaya Infusion

2 ounces Lemon Grass Syrup (see page 25)

12 ounces sweetened iced tea flavored with lemon

Lemon wheels (for garnish)

Add Cucumber–Papaya Infusion, tea, and Lemon Grass Syrup to a pitcher. Stir. Add ice to tall glasses.

Garnish with a lemon wheel and serve.

SUMMER INFUSIONS

Bing Cherry Infusion

Balanced nuttiness, blended with tart sweetness.

   9 pints pitted Bing cherries
   4 cinnamon sticks
   1 750 ml amaretto
   1 750 ml VS cognac

Place fruit and cinnamon sticks in infusion jar. Pour amaretto and cognac over the top. Save the empty liquor bottles. Let infusion rest for 14 days at room temperature. Using a funnel and a sieve, strain liquid back into bottles. Place cherries in sealed glass jar and refrigerate them for later use as garnishes on cocktails like the Old Fashioned and Manhattan.

Pirate Berries Infusion

Liven up your rum with rich berries.

   3 pints blueberries
   3 pints blackberries
   3 pints raspberries
   2 750 ml dark rum
   ½ cup Cinnamon Syrup (see page 25)

Layer berries into infusion jar. Add rum and Cinnamon Syrup. Save original liquor bottles. Let rest at room temperature for 14 days. Using a funnel and sieve, strain liquid into the original bottles. Refrigerate.

Pirate Cocktail

3 ounces Pirate Berries Infusion

3 raspberries (for garnish)

Add Pirate Berries Infusion to mixing glass. Add ice to tin. Shake well. Strain into cocktail glass.

Garnish with raspberries on a pick.

Pirate's Life Lemonade

3 ounces Pirate Berries Infusion

4 ounces lemonade

Lemon wheel (for garnish)

Fill tall glass with ice. Add Pirate Berries Infusion and lemonade. Stir well.

Garnish with a lemon wheel.

AUTUMN INFUSIONS

Savory Onion Infusion

I often use Savory Onion Infusion as a marinade for meat or a spicy addition to vodka sauce. Simply add steaks or chicken fillets to a plastic bag and cover with this infusion. Let rest overnight in refrigerator. For a savory kick, substitute this infusion instead of vodka in any vodka sauce recipe.

    4 large sweet onions (sliced)
    1 jalapeño pepper (sliced thin)
    2 green bell peppers (sliced thin)
    20 peppercorns
    2 750 ml vodka

Layer onions, jalapeño, bell pepper, and peppercorns into 3-quart glass infusion jar. Pour vodka over top. Save the liquor bottles. Let rest for 7 days at room temperature. Using a funnel and sieve, strain back into vodka bottles. Refrigerate.

Spiced Caesar

    2 ounces Savory Onion Infusion
    3 ounces Clamato juice
    Clam (for garnish)

Fill tall glass with ice. Add Savory Onion Infusion and juice. Stir.

Garnish with a fresh clam.

Fig and Pear Infusion

Combines the warm flavors and spices of the season.

4 pounds d'Anjou pears (thinly sliced)
3 pints figs (cut in half, with stems removed)
4 cinnamon sticks
10 whole cloves
2 bar spoons pumpkin pie spice
1 750 ml vodka
1 750 ml orange liqueur

Place figs and pear slices in alternate layers in 3-quart glass infusion jar. Add cinnamon sticks, cloves, and pumpkin pie spice. Pour vodka and orange liqueur over top. Save the liquor bottles. Let rest for 12 days at room temperature. Using a sieve and funnel, strain back into original bottles. Store in refrigerator.

Harvest Time

2 ounces Fig and Pear Infusion
½ ounce fresh orange juice
½ ounce Fresh Sour (see page 26)

RIM INGREDIENTS

4 bar spoons super fine sugar
¼ bar spoon cinnamon
Lime wedge
Pear slice (for garnish) (Use juice of lemon wedge on pear slice to prevent it from turning brown or oxidizing)

TO RIM THE GLASS: On a small plate, combine sugar and cinnamon. Rim the outside top of the glass with lime wedge. Roll the outside rim of the cocktail glass in sugar mixture. Set aside.

Add Fig and Pear Infusion, juice, and Fresh Sour to mixing glass. Add ice to tin. Shake well. Strain into sugar–cinnamon rimmed cocktail glass.

Garnish with a pear slice.

Fall Fizz

> 2 ounces Fig and Pear Infusion
> Splash of egg white (optional) (look for small cartons of pasteurized egg white in the dairy section)
> 2 ounces Fresh Sour (see page 26)
> 1 ounce ginger ale
> Cinnamon stick (for garnish)

To mixing glass, add Fig and Pear Infusion, egg white, if using, and Fresh Sour. Add ice to tin. Shake well. Strain into ice-filled tall glass. Top with ginger ale.

Garnish with a cinnamon stick.

WINTER INFUSIONS

Pineapple–Blood Orange Infusion

Bring home these tropical flavors to chase away the winter blues.

  3 pounds blood oranges (peeled and sliced into wedges)
  2 whole pineapples (peeled and cubed)
  10 mint sprigs
  2 750 ml vodka

Layer fruit and mint into 3-quart glass infusion jar. Save pineapple leaves to use as garnish in cocktails. Add vodka. Save liquor bottles. Let rest for 7 days at room temperature. Using a funnel and sieve, strain back into vodka bottles. Store in refrigerator.

Snow Day

  Crushed ice or fresh snow
  4 ounces Pineapple-Blood Orange Infusion (see above)
  Pineapple leaf (for garnish)

Fill a rocks glass with crushed ice. Add Pineapple–Blood Orange Infusion directly from chilled bottle.

Garnish with a pineapple leaf.

Long Weekend

  2 ounces Pineapple-Blood Orange Infusion
  ½ ounce passion fruit juice
  ½ ounce Fresh Sour (see page 26)
  Rosé champagne (for topping)

In mixing glass, add Pineapple–Blood Orange Infusion, passion fruit juice, and Fresh Sour. Add ice to tin. Shake well. Strain into a champagne flute. Top with rosé champagne.

Kiwi–Tangerine Infusion

Bright flavors with the warmth of rum.

5 pounds kiwi (peeled and sliced)
2 pounds tangerines (peeled and sliced into wedges)
2 750 ml white rum

Layer fruit into 3-quart glass infusion jar. Add rum. Save liquor bottles. Let rest at room temperature for 7 days. Using a funnel and sieve, strain into original bottles. Store in refrigerator.

Jack Frost

2 ounces Kiwi–Tangerine Infusion
½ ounce Honey Rosemary Syrup (see page 25)
2 ounces apple juice
Juice of 1 lime wedge
Kiwi slice (for garnish)

To mixing glass, add Kiwi–Tangerine Infusion, Honey Rosemary Syrup, apple juice, and juice of a lime wedge. Add ice to tin. Shake well. Strain into an ice-filled rocks glass.

Garnish with a kiwi wheel.

Monday, Monday

3 ounces Kiwi–Tangerine Infusion
Tangerine wedge (for garnish)

Add Kiwi–Tangerine Infusion to mixing glass. Add ice to tin. Shake well. Strain into an ice-filled rocks glass.

Garnish with a tangerine wedge.

Tilly's Limoncello Infusion

In honor of Great-Great Aunt Tilly, pictured at right. Aunt Tilly was the first female bartender in my family. She was a stunning woman with lavender eyes who was as sturdy as she was beautiful. She managed the family tavern in the coal-mining town of Coal City, Illinois, during an era when women were not allowed to be patrons. This infusion is dedicated to the courageous spirit of women and celebrates Tilly's Italian heritage.

Rinds of 9 large lemons
Rinds of 4 large oranges
2 vanilla beans (sliced lengthwise)
1 750 ml vodka
1 cup Simple Syrup (see page 24)
½ bar spoon cream of tartar

Add fruit rinds to 3-quart glass infusion jar. Add vanilla and pour vodka over the top. Save liquor bottle. Let rest for 3 weeks in a dark, cool location. Using a sieve and funnel, strain into original vodka bottle. Add Simple Syrup and cream of tartar. Mix well. Refrigerate.

INDEX